von Gerkan, Marg und Partner

Messe Düsseldorf

von Gerkan, Marg und Partner

Messe Düsseldorf

Herausgegeben von
Edited by
Volkwin Marg

Einführung von
Introduction by
Volkwin Marg

Prestel

München · London · New York

Halle **6**

Hall

Gedanken zur Architektur

Thoughts on Architecture

Die Halle 6 der Messe Düsseldorf hat eine Vorgeschichte, die zur Gestaltfindung des heutigen Erscheinungsbildes erheblich beigetragen hat.

Am Anfang stand 1971 die Auslagerung der alten Messe aus den schönen Ausstellungsbauten des Architekten Wilhelm Kreis von 1926 am Rande der Altstadt. Die neue Messe des Architekten Wilke am Stadtrand und in Flughafennähe galt in den 80er und 90er Jahren ausstellungstechnisch und logistisch als vorbildlich. Die mit Rücksicht auf angrenzende Villenquartiere nicht achsial, sondern frei und locker gruppierten Hallen waren ebenerdige Dunkelhallen mit einem quadratischen Stützenraster von 30 m. Die Messe wuchs und brauchte mehr Ausstellungsflächen und auch eine stützenfreie Mehrzweckhalle für besondere Massenveranstaltungen, gegebenenfalls in Verbindung mit dem Rheinstadion.

Wir präsentierten beim 1997 unter 151 Architekten veranstalteten Ideen- und Realisierungswettbewerb den Vorschlag, das Hallenareal in den Innenbereich hineinwachsen zu lassen und dort für das Publikum eine Erschließungsgalerie mit einer attraktiven neuen Adresse am Rhein anzulegen. Die neue Mehrzweckhalle sollte wie eine Arena kreisrund mit einer tensegren Filigranstruktur überwölbt und mit 160 m Durchmesser Europas größter Kuppelbau werden.

Dem Preisgericht gefielen unsere Ideen, aber der Messe als unserem Bauherrn gefiel unser Kuppelbau nicht, denn sie gab den Erfordernissen des regelmäßigen und orthogonal organisierten Ausstellungsbetriebes den Vorzug gegenüber dem ausnahmsweisen konzentrischen Arenabetrieb. So waren wir Architekten zur sprichwörtlichen Quadratur des Kreises gezwungen, wenn wir bauen wollten, und das wollten wir. Wir transformierten den runden Kuppelbau in eine von einem Raumtragwerk überdachte Quadrat-Halle mit gleichem Durchmesser von 160 m.

Die Gestaltsprache unserer Architektur erstrebt rationale Selbstverständlichkeit. Die Strukturen der konstruktiven Geometrie sind einsichtig und logisch. Im übertragenen Sinne ist uns beim architektonischen Gestalten die Vernunft, wie in der Astronomie, lieber als die Magie modischer und irrationaler Formdeutungen wie in der Astrologie.

Die Ästhetik unserer Architektur kultiviert die Wahrnehmung zweckdienlicher Technik im Ganzen wie im Detail und inszeniert das befreiende Erlebnis des weiten Raumes für die Besucher, die ihn erleben.

Volkwin Marg

Hall 6 at the Düsseldorf trade fair looks back on a long history, that to a considerable extent is responsible for the final shape and appearance of the building.

The history started in 1971, with the trade fair having to move out of the beautifully designed exhibition pavilions of 1926, built by Wilhelm Kreis close to the historic city center. In the 1980s and 1990s, the new trade fair complex, built to plans by the architect Wilke on the outskirts of Düsseldorf and near the airport, was regarded as exemplary in terms of exhibition architecture, technology and logistics. Taking care not to infringe upon the residential neighborhood, the architect arranged the pavilions not along one great axis, but as irregulary spaced groups of single-story dark halls, each based on a 30-meter-square column grid. The trade fair expanded and needed more exhibition space as well as a column-free, multi-purpose hall for special mass events in connection with the Rhine Stadium.

For the 1997 architectual competition among 151 architects, we proposed to extend the hall floor into the central area where we planned a concourse gallery open to the public as a new, attractive location on the Rhine. We also suggested a multi-purpose hall in the shape of a circular arena, vaulted over by a filigree, tensile, structure with a diameter of 160 meters, which would have made the hall the largest domed structure in Germany.

The jury favored our ideas, but the clients—the trade fair directors—did not like the dome, preferring to give priority to the smooth operations facilitated by a regular, orthogonal building, and therefore rejected our concentric arena structure. This forced us to attempt the proverbial quadrature of the circle if we wanted to build, which we did. We transformed the round dome into a square hall with the same diameter of 160 meters, spanned by a space-frame roof structure.

With our architectural language, we aim for self-evident rationality. Our structural geometry is clear and logical. In the figurative sense, in designing we prefer the logic of astronomy to the magic of the more fashionable and irrational interpretation of forms in astrology.

Our architectural aesthetic cultivates the perception of utilitarian technology—both overall and in detail—and stages the liberating experience of vast spaces for the visitor to enjoy.

Volkwin Marg

Blick auf das Messegelände
von Südwesten mit der Halle 6
vis-à-vis zum Stadion

View of the fair grounds from
the southwest with the Hall 6
opposite the stadium

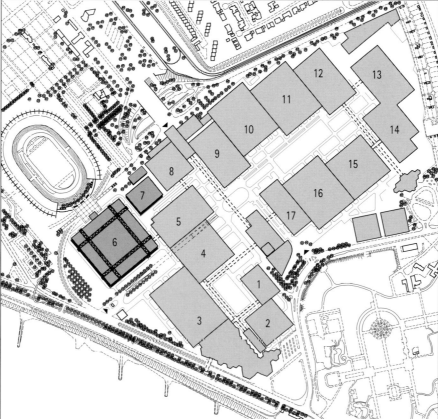

Lageplan mit den neuen
Hallen 6 und 7 und der
künftigen Stadionanbindung

Site plan with the new
Halls 6 and 7 and the future
connection to the stadium

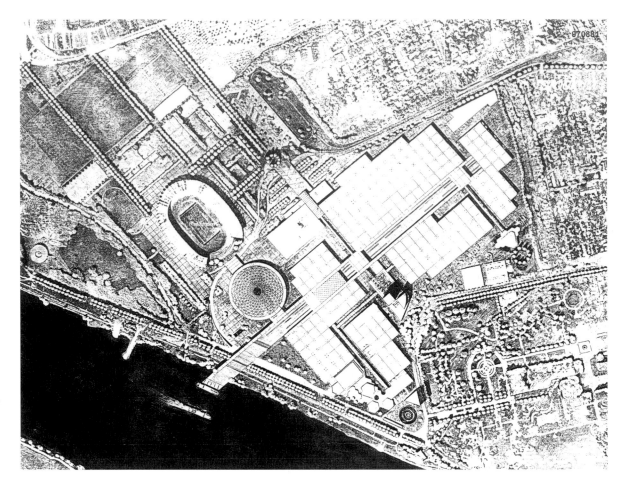

Gesamtplan des Messegeländes mit neuer Adresse am Rhein

Overall plan of the trade fair grounds with the new address on the Rhine

Düsseldorfs Messe funktioniert gut und kann noch wachsen, aber sie nutzt die einmalige Adresse am Rheinufer noch nicht optimal und entbehrt der architektonischen Signifikanz. Darum sollen künftig zwei dem Fluss zugewandte Eingänge neue Zeichen setzen:

— der neue Westeingang mit Europas größtem Kuppelbau für die Mehrzweckhalle in der Achse des Rheinstadions
— der aufgewertete Südeingang mit dem markanten Prisma des Kongresshotels am runden Fontänenbecken in der Achse des Nordparks

Das zukünftige stufenweise Wachstum der Messe richtet sich nach innen und verwandelt die heute indifferente räumliche Innenzone in eine lang gestreckte, von Kolonnaden gefasste, 60 Meter breite Agora, die der Schaustellung und der Logistik dient und von Restaurationen in der oberen ›Belle Etage‹ gesäumt wird.

Wettbewerbsmodell

Competition model

Düsseldorf's trade fair functions well and still has room to grow. Still, it does not yet take advantage of its unique address on the shores of the Rhine River, and lacks any architectural significance. Hence, two new entrances oriented towards the river are to draw attention to the facility in the future:

— the new west entrance with Europe's largest dome construction for the all-purpose hall set upon the axis of the Rhine Stadium
— the upgraded south entrance with the noteworthy prism of the Kongresshotel beside the round fountain set upon the axis of the North Park

The future step-by-step growth of the trade fair is to take place within its boundaries and will transform the current undifferentiated interior spatial zone into an elongated agora 60 meters in width that is bound by columns. It serves exhibition and logistical purposes and is enclosed by restaurants on the upper "belle étage."

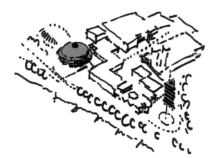

Phase 1: Zeichen setzen

– der neue Westeingang mit Europas größtem Kuppelbau für die Mehrzweckhalle in der Achse des Rheinstadions
– der aufgewertete Südeingang mit dem markanten Prisma des Kongresshotels am runden Fontänenbecken in der Achse des Nordparks

Phase 1: Setting an accent

– the new west entrance with Europe's largest dome building for a multi-purpose hall along the axis of the Rhine Stadium
– the upgraded south entrance with the striking prism of the Kongresshotel bordering the round fountain along the axis of the north park

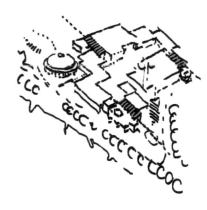

Phase 2: Eingänge stärken

– Im Zusammenhang mit den Zeichen Kuppelbau und Prisma werden die Messe-eingänge (Süd / Nord / Ost) erweitert bzw. neu definiert.
– Es ergeben sich eindeutige Eingangs-situationen und Orientierungsmöglichkeiten in die Messe-Innenzone.

Phase 2: Strengthening the entrances

– The trade fair entrances (south, north, east) are being extended or newly defined, respectively, in connection with the symbols of the dome building and the prism.
– Clear entrance areas and points of reference thus arise.

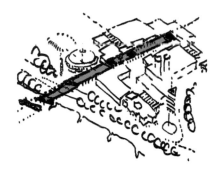

Phase 3: Brücke zum Rhein

– Die Messe-Innenzone wird durch eine umlaufende hohe Kolonnade vor den fluchtenden Hallen neu definiert.
– Über den neuen Messeeingang West und das Rhein-Plateau rückt die Messe an den Rhein.

Phase 3: The bridge to the Rhine

– The inner zone of the fair grounds is newly defined by virtue of a high, encom-passing colonnade set before the halls.
– The trade fair edges towards the Rhine by virtue of the new west entrance and the Rhine plateau.

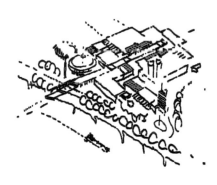

Phase 4: Messe-Wachstum

– Das zukünftige stufenweise Wachstum der Messe (bis zu 38.000m² BGF) richtet sich nach innen und verwandelt die heute räumlich indifferente Innenzone in eine lang-gestreckte Agora, die der Schaustellung und Logistik zugleich dient.

Phase 4: The growth of the trade fair

– The future, step-by-step growth of the trade fair (up to 38,000 m² gross floor area) is oriented inwardly and transforms the current undifferentiated spatial inner zone into an elongated agora that serves both exhibition and logistical purposes at once.

Die neuen Zeichen durch Licht in Szene gesetzt

The new accents are staged by means of light

7

Entwurfsüberarbeitung im Modell

Design revisions in the model

**Entwurfsüberarbeitung
Konzept und Struktur**

**Design Revisions
Concept and Structure**

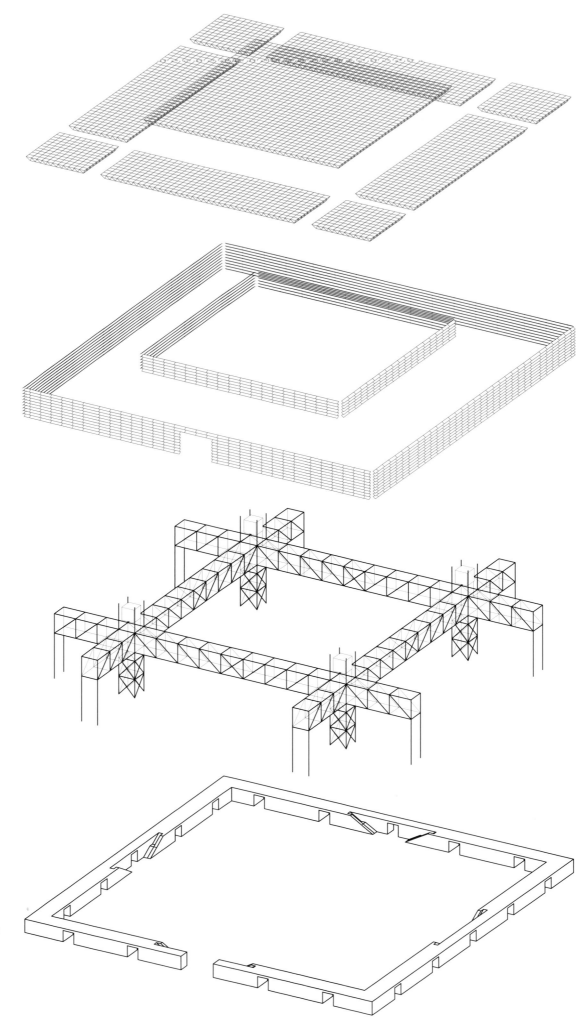

Sekundärtragwerk als
Raumtragstruktur für die
Dachflächen

Secondary superstructure
formed as a space frame
for the roof

Glasfassade mit vorgehängten
Lamellen als Sonnenschutz
und Verdunkelung

Glass façade with louvers
for sun shading and dimming
hung before it

Primärtragwerk aus Stahl-
Rundrohren

Primary superstructure made
of steel circular profiles

Ringbauwerk als massiver
Sockel zur Aufnahme der
Nebenräume und Flaniergalerie

The ring construction formed
as a solid base housing
ancillary spaces and the
pedestrian gallery

Beim Architektenwettbewerb wurde zunächst als Antwort auf das offene Oval des Stadions für die Mehrzweckhalle eine geschlossene Kreis-Kuppel vorgeschlagen, die mit 160 Metern Durchmesser Europas größte Filigrankuppel und damit eine Sensation geworden wäre.

Aber die Messe braucht eine Mehrzweckhalle, die weniger als Arena, sondern mehr als Ausstellungshalle genutzt werden soll. Bei der Entwurfsüberarbeitung erfolgte daher die Quadratur des Kreis-Grundrisses; die neue Halle bleibt aber nach wie vor ein markanter Solitär als architektonischer Gegenpol zum Stadion.

Im Messebetrieb wird die Mehrzweckhalle im Parterre an den Rundlauf der vorhandenen Messehallen angebunden, beim Veranstaltungsbetrieb wird sie auf der oberen Ebene in Höhe der umlaufenden Hallengalerie für das Publikum erschlossen, das die Halle von einem gesonderten Eingangsplateau am nördlichen Stadion betreten kann.

During the architectural competition a closed, circular dome for the multi-purpose hall 160 meters in diameter formed the first response to the open oval of the stadium. At 160 meters in diameter, Europe's largest filigree dome would have been a sensation.

But the trade fair needs a multi-purpose hall to be used less as an arena and more as an exhibition hall. Thus, the re-worked design produced a square form from the circular ground plan. The new hall remains as ever a marked solitary, acting as an architectural pole opposite the stadium.

During fair operations the multi-purpose hall is linked with the pedestrian tour of the other fair halls. During special events it is accessed by the public by the upper floor on the gallery level. The public can enter the hall from a special entrance plateau at the north stadium.

Modellaufnahme vom Innen-raum der Halle

View of the interior hall space in the model

Gesamtkonzeption

Master Concept

Im Wettbewerb der großen europäischen Messe-standorte steht Düsseldorf in der ersten Reihe – eine Positionierung, die mit der neuen Messe- und Veran-staltungshalle 6 Zukunft hat. Multifunktional, auch für Konzerte oder Sportveranstaltungen nutzbar, bildet sie den Auftakt eines Ausbaukonzeptes, das in den kommenden Jahren das Messegelände neu ordnen und modernisieren wird.

Im Gegensatz zu den bestehenden, reinen Kunstlicht-Ausstellungshallen ist die neue Halle als natürlich belichtete Mehrzweckhalle konzipiert, die je nach Bedarf durch Schließen der Außenjalousien vollständig verdunkelt werden kann. Sie ist als Teil des Messe-rundlaufs über gläserne Verbindungsbauten an die anderen Hallen erdgeschossig angebunden. Um eine ungehinderte Durchfahrt zu gewährleisten, sind die Übergänge komplett aufschiebbar. Darüber hinaus wird die neue Halle als erste Halle der Messe Düssel-dorf unabhängig vom übrigen Messegelände zu nutzen sein. Der Einlass der Besucher erfolgt dann von einer Plattform, die den Europaplatz mit dem Rheinufer verbindet. Die Plattform wird die neue Halle auch mit dem Rheinstadion verbinden. So bieten sich Möglichkeiten für eine gemeinsame Nutzung beider Anlagen.

Among the large European trade fair sites Düsseldorf ranks at the top. This can only improve in the future with the new Hall 6 for fair and special-events usage. Multifunctional in use, hosting concerts or sports events as well, it forms the beginning of an expansion concept that will newly organize and modernize the fair grounds in the years to come.

In contrast to the existing exhibition halls lit purely by artificial light, the new hall is conceived as a naturally-lit, multi-purpose hall. Depending upon the need at hand, it can be completely darkened by means of exterior louvers. It is linked with the other buildings at ground level by glass docks, and forms a part of the pedestrian tour throughout the fair grounds. In order to guarantee unencumbered passage, the transitions can be completely shifted. In addition, the new hall will be the first at Düsseldorf's fair grounds that can be used independently of the rest of the grounds. Visitors then enter via a platform that connects the Europaplatz with the shore of the Rhine. The platform will also connect the new hall with the Rhine Stadium. Thus, possibilities arise for using both facilities together.

The nearly column-free hall, with an exhibition area of 24,000 square meters, is distinguished by its simple, clear sense of spaciousness and its readable, and hence manifest, construction. The exposed steel struc-ture of the hall, measuring 160 by 160 meters, rests upon four intersecting box-girder beams that sit in turn upon four columns. The eight cantilevered ends of the box beams ease the loads upon the middle beams, which span 90 meters. To this end they are stabilized at the ends with tension columns, and are additionally loaded by the ventilation plants located upon the roof.

On the exterior, the roof connects to the lower edge of the construction, while connecting to the upper edge in the core area. Thus, varying hall heights arise with 19.5 meters (clear height 16 meters) in the encircling outer zone and 28.5 meters (clear height 26.75 meters) in the inner 90-by-90-meter zone. The suspended space frame of the ceiling takes up the aesthetically characteristic motif of the existing trade halls while offering the desired suspension points for individual loads.

Hoher und niedriger
Hallenteil am Schnittpunkt
einer Vierungs-Stütze

Upper and lower hall area
at the intersection
of a column

Fassadenstützen und
Sonnenschutzlamellen
erzeugen variable
Lichteffekte

Façade columns and
sun shading louvers
generate variable
light effects

Die nahezu stützenfreie Halle mit einer Ausstellungsfläche von 24.000 Quadratmetern zeichnet sich durch
ihre einfache, klare Großräumigkeit und ihre ablesbare
und damit sinnfällige Konstruktion aus: Die sichtbare
Stahlkonstruktion der 160 x 160 Meter messenden
Halle beruht auf vier sich kreuzenden Fachwerk-
Kasten-Trägern, die auf vier Stützen liegen. Die über-
kragenden acht Enden der Kastenträger entlasten die
90 Meter überspannenden Mittelträger. Zu diesem
Zweck sind sie an ihren Enden durch Pendelzugstützen
stabilisiert und durch die über dem Dach eingebauten
Lüftungszentralen zusätzlich belastet.

Im äußeren Bereich schließt das Dach an die Unter-
kante der Konstruktion, im Kernbereich an deren Ober-
kante an. Daraus ergeben sich die unterschiedlichen
Hallenhöhen von 19,50 Metern (lichte Höhe 16 Meter)
im umlaufenden Randbereich und 28,50 Metern
(lichte Höhe 26,75 Meter) im inneren Bereich von
90 x 90 Metern. Die eingehängten Raumtragwerke
der Decken greifen das ästhetisch prägende Motiv
der vorhandenen Messehallen auf und bieten die
gewünschten Abhängepunkte für Lasten.

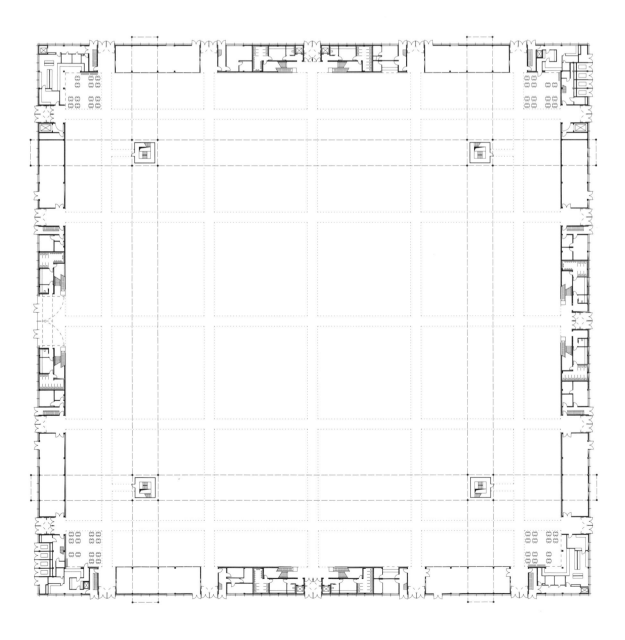

Grundrisse :
links Erdgeschoss
rechts Galeriegeschoss

Floor plans:
ground floor level left
gallery level right

14

Der taghelle Hallenraum

The hall space during the day

Der gesamte Hallenraum wird von einer sechs Meter hohen Flaniergalerie gesäumt, die nicht nur einen Blick über das Halleninnere, sondern zudem Platz für weitere Messestände, kleinere Events oder Imbiss-Stände bietet. Galerie und Halle bilden auf diese Weise eine räumliche Einheit und sind mittels Treppen, Rolltreppen, Personen- und Lastenaufzügen miteinander verbunden.

In dem darunter liegenden massiv ausgeführten Gebäudering sind die Nebenräume der Halle wie Sanitär- und Lagerräume, Informationstresen und Diensträume untergebracht. In den vier Hallenecken liegen die Restaurants mit jeweils 75 Sitzplätzen. In einem Zwischengeschoss des Ringbauwerks können Büro- und Konferenzräume von Ausstellern angemietet werden. Die mobile, voll einschiebbare Tribünenanlage, die auf 36 Reihen ca. 12000 Besuchern Platz bietet, wird von einem Teil der Lagerräume aufgenommen.

Das Organisationsraster mit jeweils achsialen Fahrstraßen, Fluchttoren und begehbaren Versorgungskanälen beträgt 30 x 30 Meter. Die Versorgung der Messestände mit Strom, Wasser, Druckluft, Telekommunikation und Datenleitungen erfolgt über im Hallenboden verlaufende Medienkanäle im Abstand von fünf Metern.

The entire hall space is surrounded by a six-meter high pedestrian gallery, which not only offers a view across the interior of the hall, but also offers space for additional fair stands, smaller events, or snack stands. The gallery and the hall thus form a spatial unit and are connected by means of stairs, escalators, passenger elevators and service elevators.

The ancillary spaces of the hall, such as rest rooms, storage rooms, information counters and service rooms, are located below the hall in the building ring, which is solid in construction. Restaurants are located in the four corners of the hall and seat 75 guests each. Office and conference spaces located within a mezzanine level of the ring area can be rented by trade exhibitors. The portable seating docks, which offer approximately 12,000 visitors space in 36 rows, are housed within a part of the storage rooms.

The organizational grid, with axial streets, egress gates and reinforced service ducts is 30 by 30 meters in size. Services to the stands for electricity, water, compressed air, telecommunications and data transfer cables are provided by media ducts located every five meters in the floor of the hall.

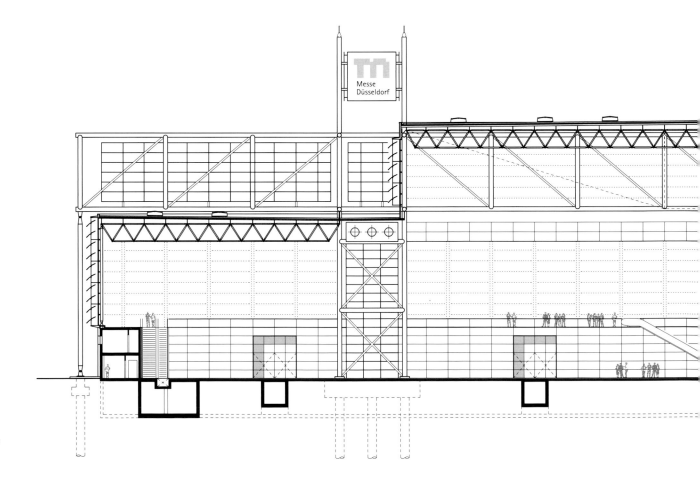

Schnitt durch die Halle
(quer zu den Versorgungs-
kanälen im Untergeschoss)

Section through the hall
(perpendicular to the supply
ducts in the lower level)

Südwestseite der Halle mit dem
Rheinstadion im Hintergrund

Southwest side of the hall
with the Rhine Stadium in the
background

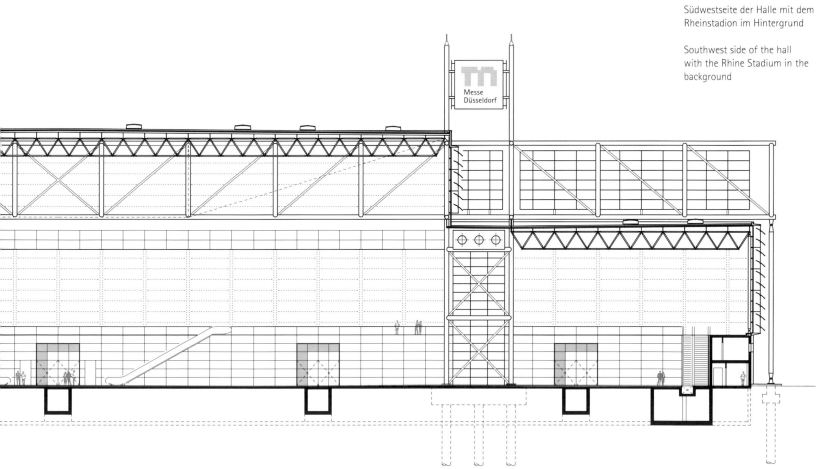

Galerieebene

Gallery level

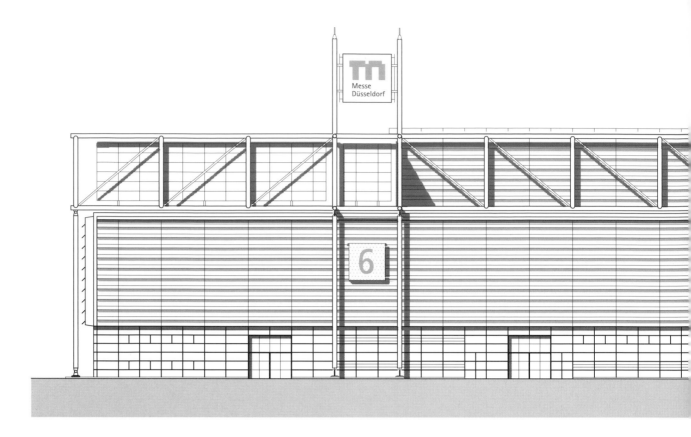

Südwestfassade mit
Big-Willi-Großtoranlage

Southwest façade with the
great Big Willi Gate

Neben der raumlufttechnischen Versorgung mit kon-
ditionierter Luft aus den Lüftungszentralen auf dem
Dach ist der Hallenraum für Sport-, Sprach- und
Konzertveranstaltungen auch akustisch vorbereitet.
Die gesamte Hallendecke sowie die Wandverkleidun-
gen des inneren Sockelbauwerks und der Stützen sind
schallabsorbierend ausgebildet.

Jede der vier Hallenseiten verfügt über fünf verglaste
Einfahrtstore; an der dem Rhein zugewandten Südwestseite ist eines davon als 15 x 16 Meter großes
Sondertor ausgebildet. Damit wird die Bestückung
der Halle z.B. mit großen Schiffen für die jährlich
stattfindende ›Boot‹ sichergestellt. Neben der An-
dienung der Halle mit Sattelschleppern während der
Auf- und Abbauphasen erfolgt über die 5 x 5 Meter
großen, verglasten Hallentore auch die Erschließung
für die Hallenbesucher.

Die konzeptionelle Nutzungsgliederung in Ringbauwerk und Hallenraum ist auch an der äußeren Fassa-
dengestaltung ablesbar. Das Sockelbauwerk ist mit
wärmegedämmten Aluminiumkassetten verkleidet.
Die eigentlichen Hallenfassaden darüber sind vollständig verglast und können mittels vorgehängter
Verschattungslamellen aus Aluminium verdunkelt
werden. Auf diese Weise verwandelt sich die Tageslichthalle auf Wunsch in eine Blackbox.

Besides the conditioned air drawn from the ventilation plants on the roof, the hall is also acoustically
designed to house sports, vocal, and concert events.
The entire roof of the hall as well as the wall claddings
of the inner base and the columns, are acoustically
absorbent.

Each of the four sides of the hall is provided with
five glazed entrance gates. One of the gates facing
the Rhine on the southwest side is formed as a
special gate 15 by 16 meters in size. Thus, the hall
can accommodate sizeable objects such as large boats
for the yearly boat fair. While the 5-by-5-meter glass
gates receive tractor-trailers during setup and break-
down phases they also serve as visitor entrances.

The conceptual organization into the ring space and
the hall space, reflecting the building's usage, can also
be read in the design of the exterior façade. The base
is clad with insulated aluminum cassettes. The actual
hall façades above the base are completely glazed
and can be darkened by means of aluminum shading
louvers hung before them. In this way, the daylighted
hall can be transformed at will into a black box.

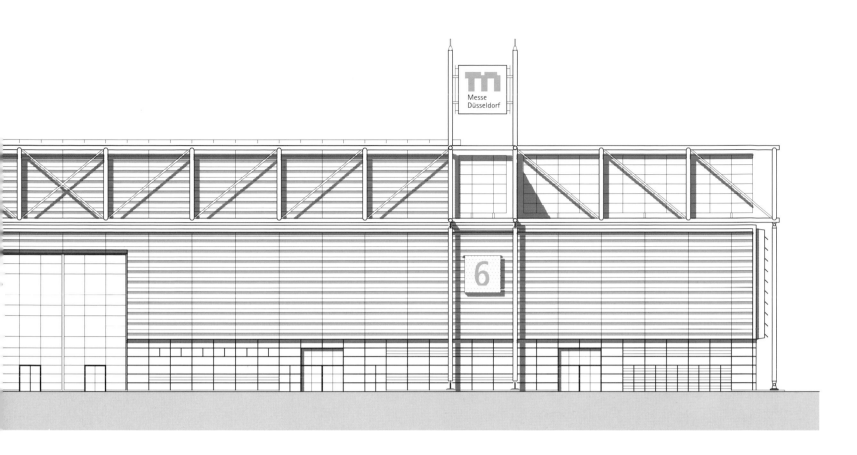

Die Pendelzugstützen sind
lesbares konstruktives Gliede-
rungselement der Fassaden.

The hinged tension columns
are a readable, constructive
element of articulation in the
façades.

Tragwerk

Superstructure

Das stählerne Dachtragwerk gliedert sich in eine Primär- und Sekundärkonstruktion. Die Primärkonstruktion besteht aus vier parallelgurtigen Fachwerkträgern, die in den Kreuzungspunkten von kräftigen, fachwerkartigen Stützen, an ihren auskragenden Enden von schlanken Zugpendeln getragen werden. Zusammen mit der ›Ballastierung‹ durch die 70 t schweren Lüftungsaggregate auf den Auskragungen kann die Biegebeanspruchung im Innenfeld erheblich reduziert werden. Als Sekundärkonstruktion wurde, wie schon in den bestehenden Messehallen, ein Raumfachwerksystem gewählt, das die Dachhaut trägt.

Die Fachwerkträger bestehen aus Rohrprofilen, die steifenlos miteinander verschweißt sind. Für die Gurte und Pfosten wurden Rohrprofile ø 508 x 6,3 mm bis 50 mm, in den am höchsten beanspruchten Knotenbzw. Lasteinleitungsbereichen auch Vollmaterial ø 508 mm und für die Diagonalen Rohrprofile ø 193,7 x 5,6 mm bis 32 mm verwendet. Die im Vergleich zu den Gurten dünnen Diagonalen wirken wie Stangen und zeigen damit ihre statische Funktion als ausschließlich normalkraftbeanspruchte Bauteile. Eine ausreichende horizontale Aussteifung gegenüber Windlasten auf die oberen Fassaden wurde durch Diagonalen in der Ober- und Untergurtebene erreicht.

Die gesamte Primärkonstruktion ist ohne verschiebliche Lager ausgeführt, d.h. Fachwerkträger und Innenstützen sind vollverschweißt und die Fußpunkte der Innenstützen sind mit Spanngliedern an die Pfahlkopfplatte fest angeschlossen. Dies hat den Vorteil, dass die recht großen temperaturbedingten Horizontalverschiebungen in alle Richtungen gleich groß sind, da sich der Ruhepunkt genau in der Hallenmitte befindet. Dehnfugen an Fassaden und Dachhaut konnten damit in jedem Quadranten gleich ausgebildet werden, und dem Tragwerk wurde zusätzliche Redundanz verliehen.

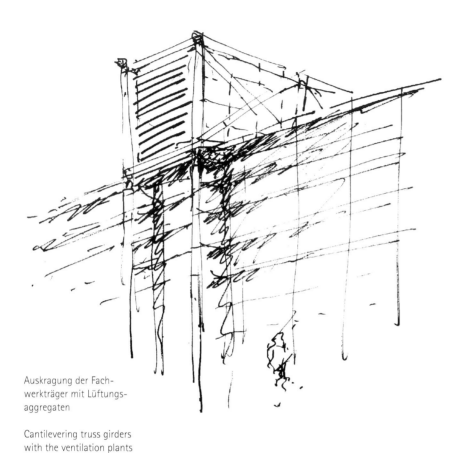

Auskragung der Fachwerkträger mit Lüftungsaggregaten

Cantilevering truss girders with the ventilation plants

Schnittmodell

Sectional model

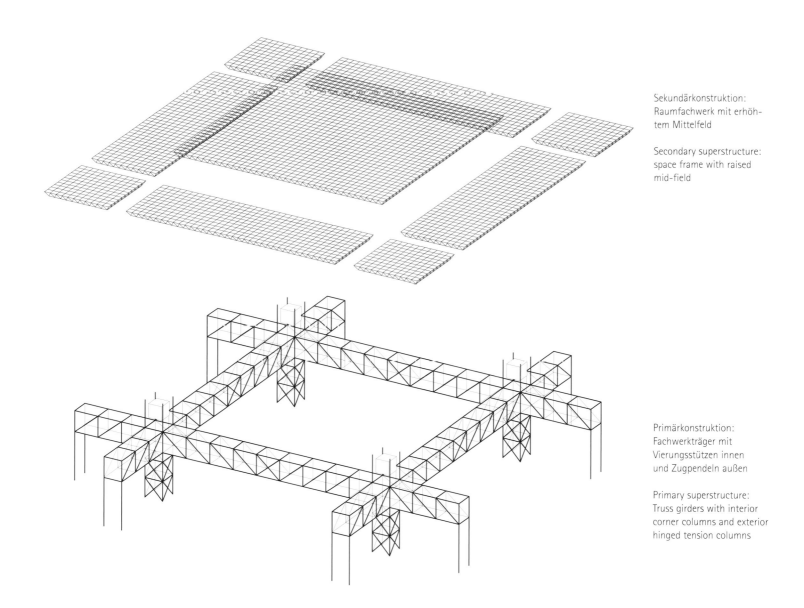

Sekundärkonstruktion:
Raumfachwerk mit erhöh-
tem Mittelfeld

Secondary superstructure:
space frame with raised
mid-field

Primärkonstruktion:
Fachwerkträger mit
Vierungsstützen innen
und Zugpendeln außen

Primary superstructure:
Truss girders with interior
corner columns and exterior
hinged tension columns

Zur Primärkonstruktion gehört auch die Unterspannung für das 90 x 90 m große Innenfeld. Sie trägt das Dach über vier Luftstützen aus Rohrprofilen ø 508 x 20 mm und begrenzt somit die Stützweite für das darüber liegende Raumfachwerk wie in den Seitenfeldern auf maximal 30 m. Um zu große Durchbiegungen, vor allem in Hinblick auf die Entwässerung, zu vermeiden, wurden keine hochfesten Seile, sondern steifere Stangen aus Vergütungsstahl 42CrMo4 eingesetzt. Aufgrund der außerordentlich hohen Kräfte wurden die Zugstangen jeweils paarweise angeordnet und für die Diagonalen erstmals ø M 176 eingesetzt. Fertigungsbedingt mussten die 42 m langen Diagonalen mit zwei Schraubmuffen und einem Spannschloss gestoßen werden. Zur Horizontalaussteifung wurden zusätzlich Diagonalen kreuzweise angeordnet. Alle Zugglieder haben Gabelköpfe und sind über Augenbleche angeschlossen. An den Luftstützen und den vier Anschlusspunkten an die Primärkonstruktion wurden die Hohlprofile durch Vollmaterial ersetzt. Damit können die aus unterschiedlichen Richtungen angreifenden hohen Zugkräfte ideal kurzgeschlossen werden.

Das etwa 27.000 Stäbe umfassende Raumfachwerk (System ›Krupp-Montal‹) bildet die Sekundärkonstruktion. Es hat ein Grundrissraster von 2,50 m und liegt im Abstand von 10 m auf den vier Fachwerkträgern bzw. den umlaufend angeordneten Fassadenstützen auf. Die Lasten aus dem Raumfachwerk werden über vier sternförmig angeordnete Auflagerpunkte in die Luftstützen eingeleitet. Das Raumfachwerk besteht aus Rohrprofilen ø 70 x 2,3 mm bis ø 177,8 x 8 mm (aus Stahl S 235, S 355), die in den Knoten verschraubt sind.

Detailentwicklung bis zum ausgeführten Knotenpunkt

Detail development up to the executed node

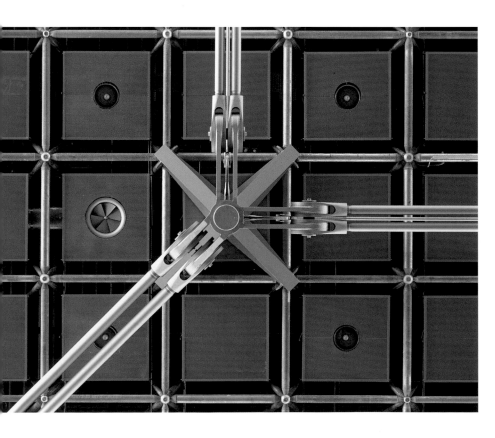

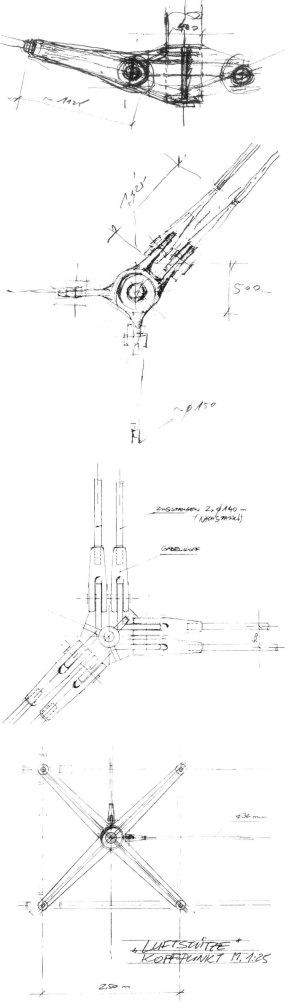

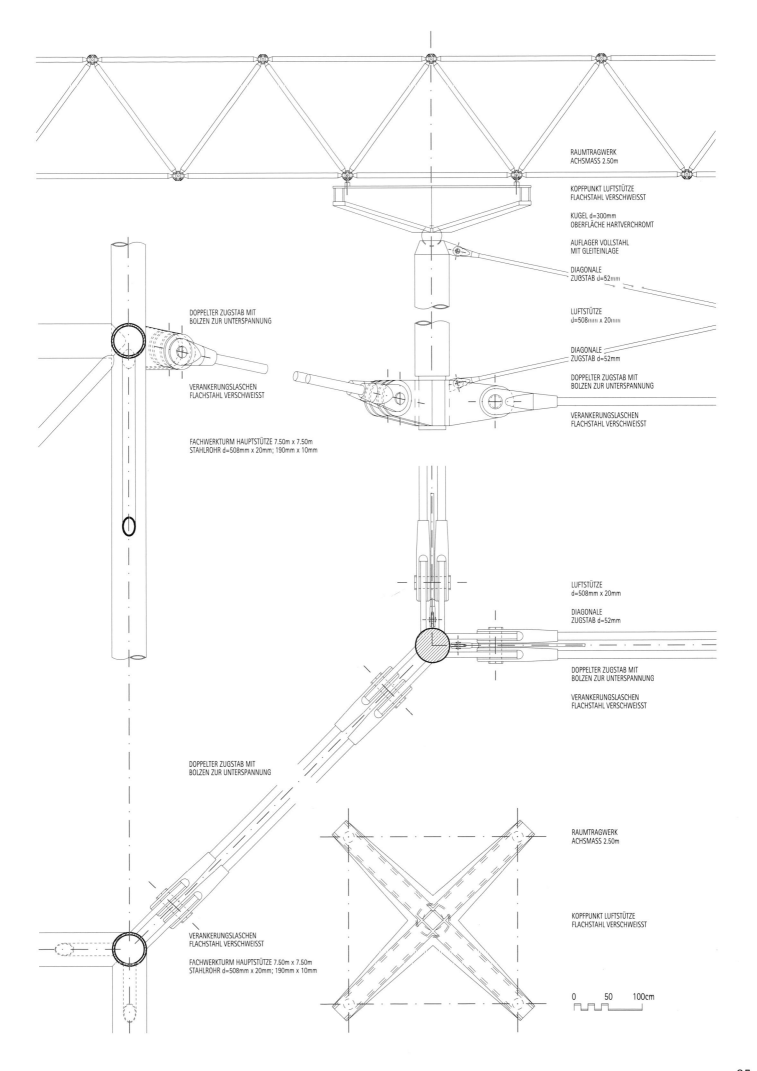

RAUMTRAGWERK
ACHSMASS 2.50m

KOPFPUNKT LUFTSTÜTZE
FLACHSTAHL VERSCHWEISST

KUGEL d=300mm
OBERFLÄCHE HARTVERCHROMT

AUFLAGER VOLLSTAHL
MIT GLEITEINLAGE

DIAGONALE
ZUGSTAB d=52mm

LUFTSTÜTZE
d=508mm x 20mm

DIAGONALE
ZUGSTAB d=52mm

DOPPELTER ZUGSTAB MIT
BOLZEN ZUR UNTERSPANNUNG

VERANKERUNGSLASCHEN
FLACHSTAHL VERSCHWEISST

DOPPELTER ZUGSTAB MIT
BOLZEN ZUR UNTERSPANNUNG

VERANKERUNGSLASCHEN
FLACHSTAHL VERSCHWEISST

FACHWERKTURM HAUPTSTÜTZE 7.50m x 7.50m
STAHLROHR d=508mm x 20mm; 190mm x 10mm

LUFTSTÜTZE
d=508mm x 20mm

DIAGONALE
ZUGSTAB d=52mm

DOPPELTER ZUGSTAB MIT
BOLZEN ZUR UNTERSPANNUNG

VERANKERUNGSLASCHEN
FLACHSTAHL VERSCHWEISST

DOPPELTER ZUGSTAB MIT
BOLZEN ZUR UNTERSPANNUNG

RAUMTRAGWERK
ACHSMASS 2.50m

KOPFPUNKT LUFTSTÜTZE
FLACHSTAHL VERSCHWEISST

VERANKERUNGSLASCHEN
FLACHSTAHL VERSCHWEISST

FACHWERKTURM HAUPTSTÜTZE 7.50m x 7.50m
STAHLROHR d=508mm x 20mm; 190mm x 10mm

0   50   100cm

Die Fassadenstützen sind gelenkig gelagert, tragen also die Windlast je zur Hälfte in ihren Fußpunkt sowie in das Raumfachwerk ab. Dadurch waren schlanke Rohrprofile ø 323,9 mm und gestalterisch ansprechende Fußpunkte möglich. In den Seitenfeldern wirkt das Raumfachwerk als liegender Biegeträger. Damit werden die Fachwerkträger der Primärkonstruktion durch Wind auf die untere Fassade nur unwesentlich beansprucht.

Trotz der ungewöhnlich hohen Lasten der Lüftungstechnik (allein 560 t für die acht Lüftungsaggregate) sowie der hohen Zusatzlasten des Veranstaltungsbetriebs (Flächenlast von bis zu 110 kg/m^2 ungünstig auf ein Fünftel der Dachfläche) konnte ein filigranes Dach mit einem Konstruktionsgewicht von nur 73 kg/m^2 realisiert werden, dessen Tragwerk nicht nur integraler Bestandteil ist, sondern als solches auch eigenständig in Erscheinung tritt.

Dr.-Ing. Michael Pötzl

Luftstütze

Column

Blick in die Diagonale der Halle

Diagonal view through the hall

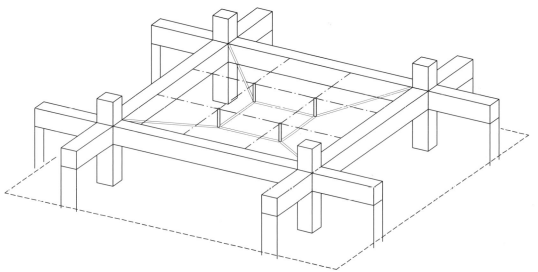

Unterspannungsschema des
90 x 90 m großen Innenfeldes

Cable support plan for the
90-by-90-meter interior field

The load bearing, steel roof structure is divided into a primary and a secondary structure. The primary structure consists of four parallel-cord trusses that are supported at their intersections by sturdy, space-frame-like columns. The cantilevered ends of the trusses are attached to slim tension elements. Together with the "ballasting" by means of the 70-ton ventilation plants on the cantilevers, the bending stress in the inner field can be substantially reduced. A space frame system, which supports the roof skin and which can already be found in the existing fair halls, was chosen as the secondary structure.

The trusses are made of circular hollow sections welded together without any stiffening. For the chords and posts, sections were chosen with a diameter of 508 mm and a wall thickness ranging from 6.3 mm to 50 mm. For the joints or, respectively, the load distribution zones with the highest loads, solid sections were chosen with the same diameter. The circular sections for the diagonals were sized at 193.7 mm with a wall thickness between 5.6 mm and 32 mm. The diagonal members, which appear comparatively thin next to the chords, appear rod-like and thus exhibit their static function as building elements with an absolutely normal load-bearing function. A sufficient horizontal rigidity for wind loads on the upper façade was achieved by means of diagonal members on the upper and lower chord levels.

The entire primary structure is executed without sliding bearings. Thus, trusses and the interior columns are welded solidly together and the bases of the interior columns are solidly connected by tendons to the heads of the foundation piles. This has the advantage of distributing the large, temperature-related horizontal expansion evenly in every direction, since the point of equilibrium is located precisely at the center of the hall. Expansion joints on the façade and in the roof skin could thus be made identical in every quadrant, while lending the structural system additional redundancy.

The cable supporting for the 90-by-90-meter inner field belongs to the primary structure as well. It supports the roof via four columns made of circular hollow sections 508 mm in diameter and 20 mm thick. This thus limits the bearing distance to a maximum of 30 meters for the space frame located above as well as in the side fields. In order to avoid excessive deflection, above all with regard to water drainage, 42CrMo4 tempered steel rods are used instead of less stiff high-tensile cable. Because of the extraordinarily high loads, the tension rods were supplied in pairs and sized for the first time with an M 176 diameter. For manufacturing reasons the 42-meter-long diagonal members had to be assembled in parts and joined by two bolt sleeves and a turnbuckle. Additional cross-laid diagonal members were added in order to provide horizontal rigidity. All tension members have open spelter pockets and are connected by lugs. The hollow sections were replaced by solid sections at the columns and at the four intersections. In this manner, the high tensile loads originating from different directions can be optimally neutralized.

Primärtragwerk im Aufbau

Primary superstructure
under construction

The space frame, which consists of about 27,000 rods ("Krupp-Montal" system) forms the secondary structure. It has a ground plan grid of 2.5 meters and sits upon the four trusses every 10 meters or the encircling façade columns, respectively. The loads from the space frame are directed into the columns via four star-like bearing points. The space frame consists of hollow sections ranging from 70 mm in diameter and 2.3 mm thick, to 177.8 mm in diameter and 8 mm thick (in S235 and S355 steel) that are bolted together at their nodes.

The columns of the façade are articulated at their joints, thus directing half of the wind loads through their base and half through the space frame. Hence, slim hollow sections (323.9 mm in diameter) were able to be employed and an attractive base design was achieved. The space frame in the sidefields acts as a horizontal beam under bending. Thus, the girders of the primary structure are only minimally called upon to carry wind loads bearing upon the lower façade.

Despite the extraordinarily high loads from the ventilation equipment (560 tons alone for the eight ventilation plants), as well as the additional high loads brought by entertainment operations (area loads of up to 110 kg/m^2 adversely distributed upon one fifth of the roof area), a filigree roof design weighing only 73 kg/m^2 was able to be built. Its structure is not only an inherent part of the roof, but also appears as a sovereign element in and of itself.

Dr. Michael Pötzl, Engineer

Aufstellen der
Primärkonstruktion

Assembling the
primary superstructure

Montage des
Sekundärtragwerks

Assembling the
secondary superstructure

31

Fassade

Façade

Für die Halle 6 wurden speziell entwickelte drehbare Verschattungs- und Verdunkelungslamellen verwendet und damit der Prototyp einer komplett verdunkelbaren Messe- und Veranstaltungshalle geschaffen. Die Nutzungsgliederung in weiträumige Halle mit Galerie und dienendem Ringbauwerk ist in der architektonischen Gestaltung der Fassade ablesbar:

Das Sockelbauwerk ist mit gekanteten Aluminiumblechen verkleidet. Schattenfugen und kantige Schwerter im Raster von 1,00 x 2,50 Metern gliedern den gesamten Sockel. Fenster, Lüftungslamellenbänder, Alukassetten und Türen sind in dieses Raster integriert.

Die eigentliche Hallenfassade ist als Pfosten-Riegel-Konstruktion mit Aluminiumprofilen konzipiert. Stützen auf der Galerie im Abstand von fünf Metern nehmen die Kräfte der riesigen Glasfläche auf. Durch das System der außen liegenden Verschattungselemente konnte auf Sonnenschutzglas verzichtet werden.

Die vorgehängte Sekundärstruktur für die beweglichen Sonnenschutzlamellen mit Reinigungs- und Wartungsumgängen ist als verzinkte Stahlkonstruktion ausgebildet. Die Lamellen bestehen aus extrudiertem Aluminium und sind aus jeweils fünf Teilen zusammengesteckt. Linearmotoren mit paarweiser Koppelung treiben die 5 bzw. 7,50 Meter langen und 1,20 Meter hohen Lamellen über Gestänge an.

Je nach Sonnenstand und -intensität wird über zehnstufig voreinstellbare Neigungswinkel einerseits die Blendfreiheit in der Halle, andererseits der freie Ausblick in den Himmel garantiert.

Die obere Laternenfassade ist wie die Glasfassade der Halle mit Sonnenschutzlamellen ausgestattet und belichtet den inneren hohen Hallenraum.

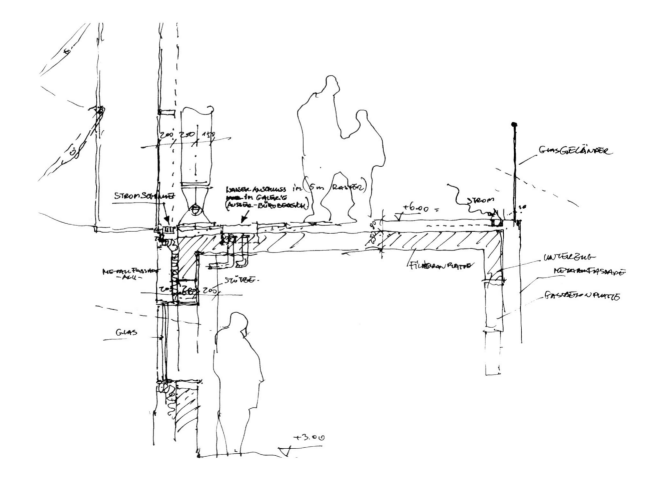

Konzeptskizze zur Galerie

Conceptual sketch
for the gallery

32

For the Hall 6 specially-developed, rotating shading and dimming louvers were put to use, thus creating the prototype for a fair and concert hall that can be completely darkened.

The articulation of the spacious hall with its gallery and service ring, reflecting the usage within, can be read in the architectural design of the façade. The base is clad with folded aluminum panels. Shadow joints and swords at a grid of 1.0 by 2.5 meters articulate the entire base. Windows, ventilation grates, aluminum cassettes and doors are integrated into the grid.

The actual façade of the hall is designed as a post and beam system with aluminum sections. Columns on the gallery spaced every five meters carry the load of the enormous glass surface. Because of the exterior shading elements, sun-shading glass did not need to be employed.

The secondary curtain wall structure for the adjustable sun-shading louvers, with its window washing and service catwalks, is constructed with galvanized steel. The louvers are made of extruded aluminum and are joined together as five-part units. Rods attached to linear motors coupled in pairs drive the louvers, which are 5.0 or 7.5 meters in length and 1.2 meters in height. Depending upon the elevation and intensity of the sun the amount of glare in the hall on the one hand, as well as the unfettered view to the outside on the other hand, can be controlled by the 10-step, variable-angle louver settings.

The upper lantern façade, like the glass façade of the hall, is equipped with sun-shading louvers and illuminates the high inner space of the hall.

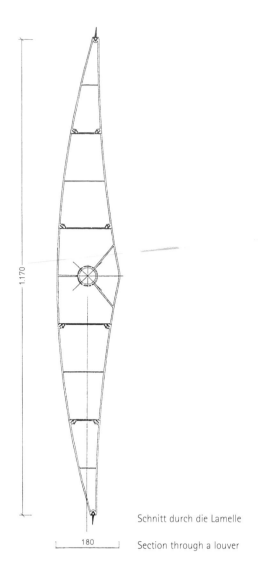

1.170

180

Schnitt durch die Lamelle

Section through a louver

Detailansicht von innen

Interior detail elevation

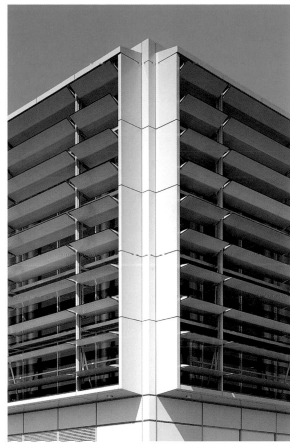

Offenes und geschlossenes
Lamellenfeld

Gebäudeecke

Open and closed louver field

Building corner

Wartungs- und
Reinigungsgang im
Fassadenzwischenraum

Maintenance and window-
washing catwalk within the
façade cavity

35

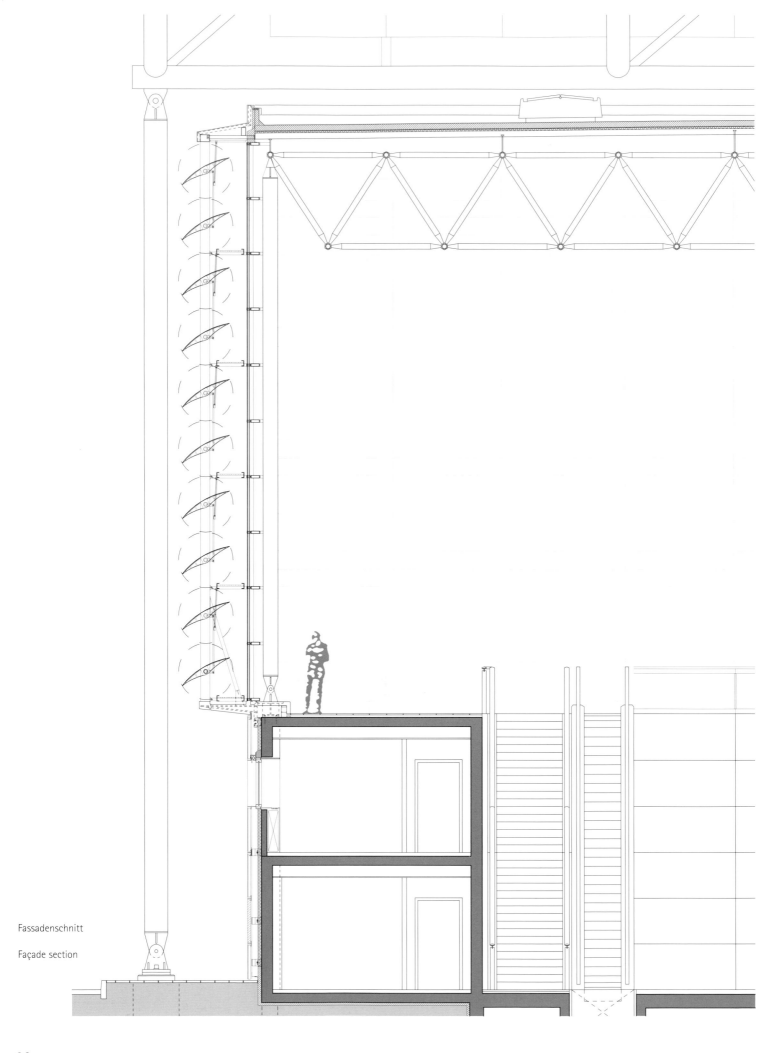

Fassadenschnitt

Façade section

Fußpunkt Fassadenstütze
auf dem Galeriesockel

Base of a façade column
upon the gallery base

Hallenzugang als verglaste
Drehflügel-Toranlage

Hall access as a glazed
pivot gate

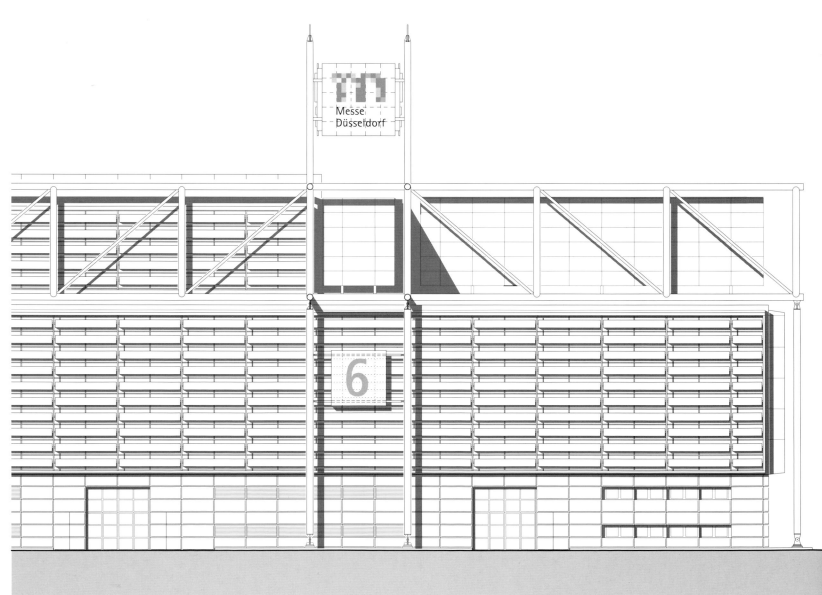

Südwestfassade mit
Großtor Big Willi

Southwest façade with
the great Big Willi Gate

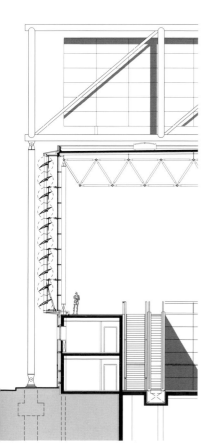

Ansicht und Schnitt der Halle

Elevation and section
through the hall

Hallennummerierung

The Hall Number

Neonbeleuchtung
der Hallennummer

Neon lighting
of the hall number

Für eine auf der Außenwand befestigte Hallennummer mußte aufgrund der beweglichen Fassade der Halle 6 eine Sonderlösung gefunden werden. Die Idee, das Sichtbare auf die eigentliche Ziffer zu reduzieren, führte zu einer transparenten Unterkonstruktion aus extrudiertem Acrylglas.

Zwei zwischen den Pendelstützen des Primärtragwerks eingehängte Rohre tragen die 25 mm dünne, zweigeteilte Scheibe mit den Abmessungen von 4,20 x 4,20 Metern. Eigengewicht und Windlasten werden über vier stehende, 500 mm breite Acrylglas-Schwerter abgetragen, die mit den Scheiben schubfest verbunden sind. Durch diese ›gläsernen Rippen‹ wurde die Wirkung einer scheinbar schwebenden Scheibe mit einer Fläche von insgesamt 17 m² erreicht. Zur zusätzlichen Sicherung sind die Scheiben an den beiden Querrohren punktförmig gehalten. Die Beleuchtung des drei Meter hohen Ziffernkörpers erfolgt über mundgeblasene Neonumfahrungen.

A special solution for Hall 6 had to be found for the number attached to the exterior of its moveable façade. The idea of reducing the visible element to the actual digit itself led to a transparent subconstruction made of extruded acrylic glass.

Two pipe sections hung between the hinged tension columns of the primary superstructure support the 25-mm-thick, two-part sheet measuring 4.2 by 4.2 meters. Its own weight and wind loads are carried by four vertical, 500-mm-wide acrylic glass swords rigidly connected to the sheets. The effect of a seemingly floating sheet with an area of 17 m² was reached with the help of these "glass ribs." For additional safety the sheets are attached to both of the lateral sections at single points. The three-meter-high numbers are illuminated by hand-blown neon tubing.

Schattenspiel auf den
verstellbaren Lamellen

Play of shadows
on the adjustable louvers

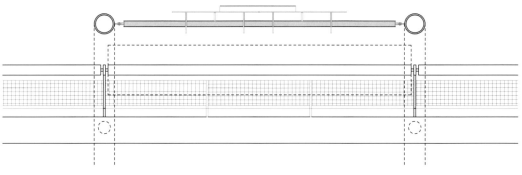

Ansicht und Schnitte
zur Nummerierung

Elevation and section
of the numbering

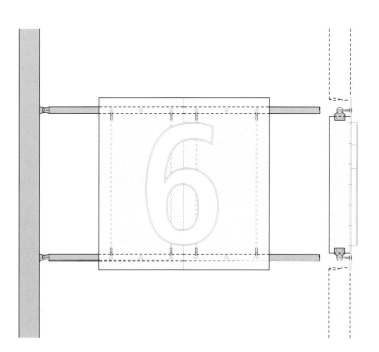

Großtoranlage
Big Willi

The Great
Big Willi Gate

In der Mittelachse der Südwestfassade gibt das Großtor Big Willi den Blick zur offenen Rheinlandschaft
frei. Das lichtdurchlässige Tor überwindet die Zwei-
teilung der unterschiedlichen Fassadenstrukturen
von Sockelbauwerk und Hallenraum und verschmilzt
sie miteinander.

Segeljachten und Motorboote werden anlässlich
der ›Boot‹ vom Portalkran Big Willi aus dem Rhein
gehoben und anschließend mit Tiefladern durch das
zweiflügelige Drehtor in die Halle gebracht. Mit einer
Breite von 15 Metern und einer Höhe von 15,8 Metern
ist das Big-Willi-Tor weltweit eines der größten Tore
dieser Bauart. Der 29 t schwere Torkörper besteht
aus einer Rohr-Rahmenkonstruktion mit den Abmessungen 300 x 200 mm und einer vorgesetzten,
eigens entwickelten Pfosten-Riegel-Konstruktion für
die Glasfassade.

Bevor sich die Torflügel in den Hallenraum öffnen,
wird die Hebebrücke, welche die Galerie miteinander
verbindet, hochgefahren. Die Tore werden auf zwei
in den Hallenboden eingelassenen Edelstahlschienen
geführt und über jeweils einen Flurantrieb bewegt.

The great Big Willi Gate along the middle axis of
the southwest façade offers a view out to the open
Rhine landscape. The translucent gate bridges the
two-part division of the different structures of the
base and the hall, melting them into one.

For the "Boot" exhibition, sailing yachts and motor
boots are lifted out of the Rhine by the Big Willi
port crane and then brought through the double-door
gate into the hall by low-riding transporters. With
a width of 15 meters and a height of 15.8 meters, the
Big Willi Gate is one of the largest gates of its kind
throughout the world. The 29-ton gate is made with
a pipe frame construction, whose sections measure
300 by 200 mm, and a customized post and beam
system hung before it for the glass façade.

Before the doors of the gate can open up into the hall
the drawbridge, which connects the gallery, must be
raised. The gates ride upon two stainless steel tracks
sunk into the floor of the hall and are each propelled
by a separate drive unit.

Toröffnung bei
hochgeklappter Brücke

Opening the gate with the
bridge in the raised position

Big-Willi-Brücke

The Big Willi Bridge

Vor dem Big-Willi-Tor verbindet eine 15 Meter lange und 2,25 Meter breite Brücke aus Stahl die umlaufende Galerie. Ihre Planung wurde notwendig, weil sich das Großtor wegen seiner immensen Windangriffsfläche von mehr als 230 Quadratmetern nur in den geschützten Hallenraum öffnen ließ.

Die Hebebrücke besteht aus zwei Hälften, die über Hubzylinder so aufgeklappt werden können, dass der gesamte Lichtraum des Tores zur Verfügung steht. Im geschlossenen Zustand wirken diese Hubzylinder als Unterstützung für den Überbau, der dadurch besonders schlank ausgebildet werden konnte. Vouten zur Verstärkung wurden nur nach statischer Erfordernis am Auge des hydraulischen Hubstempels ausgebildet.

Als Belag dient ein leichter Gitterrost mit Blechabdeckung. Das filigrane Geländer mit punktgeschweißten Drahtgitter-Elementen ist mit seinen Pfosten direkt an die Querträger des Überbaus angeschlossen, so dass insgesamt eine optisch und gewichtsmäßig minimierte Konstruktion entstand.

A 15-meter-long and 2.25-meter-wide steel bridge connects the gallery that passes by the Big Willi Gate. Because of the potentially immense wind load on the gate, which measures more than 230 m² in area, it could only be opened inwardly into the protected hall, thus necessitating the design of a drawbridge.

The drawbridge is made of two halves that are raised by two pneumatic pistons, thus allowing the gate to completely pass by. In their closed position the pistons act as supports for the bridge, thus allowing its members to be sized quite slenderly. Reinforcing staunches were applied to the hub of the hydraulic shaft only as needed statically.

A light steel grating with a metal sheet cover serves as flooring. The delicate railing with spot-welded wire mesh elements is connected at its posts to the crossbeams of the bridge, such that as a whole a design was attained that is both visually satisfying and minimal in weight.

Big-Willi-Tor mit Hebebrücke
in den verschiedenen
Phasen des Hochfahrens

The Big Willi Gate with the
drawbridge in various stages
of being raised

Ansicht mit Funktionsweise
der Brücke

Elevation with functional
diagram of the bridge

Hochgeklappte Brücke

Raised bridge

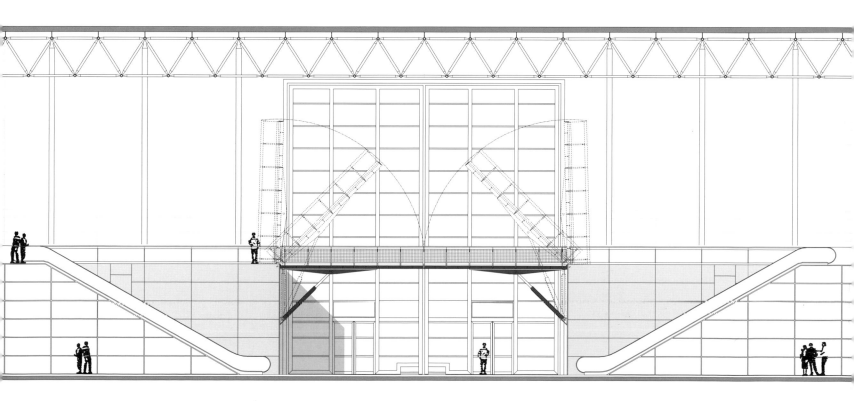

**Rolltreppen
und Aufzüge**

**Escalators
and Elevators**

Die umlaufende Galerie der Halle ist als integrierter
Bestandteil in das Hallenkonzept mit eingebunden.
Sie dient bei Veranstaltungen als Eingangs- und
Verteilerebene, die von der künftigen Plattform
zwischen Halle und Rheinstadion erschlossen wird,
und sie ist als Ausstellungsgalerie für Messestände
ausgelegt. Darüber hinaus kann die Galerie auch
als Verweil- und Pausenfläche mit gastronomischer
Versorgung genutzt werden.

Um eine optimale und gleichmäßige Anbindung
zwischen Galerie und Halle sicherzustellen, sind an
jeder der vier Seiten zwei Rolltreppenanlagen angeordnet. Sie sind gestalterisch in die Innenfassade
integriert und mit den metallischen Akustikpaneelen
der Wand verkleidet.

Die für den Personen- und Lastentransport not-
wendigen Aufzüge sind auf der Galerie gläsern
ausgebildet.

The gallery surrounding the hall is an integral element
in the concept of the hall. It serves as an entrance
and distribution level for special events and will be
connected to the future platform between the hall
and the Rhine Stadium. The gallery is also designed
as an exhibition area for trade fair stands, while
serving beyond that as a rest and meeting area with
restaurant service.

In order to guarantee an optimal and constant
connection between the gallery and the hall, two
escalators are built in at each of the four building
sides. They are integrated into the design of the interior façade and are clad with metal acoustical panels
borrowed from the wall.

The required passenger and service elevators are clad
in glass on the gallery level.

Rolltreppe und Treppe
als integrierter Bestandteil
des Ringbauwerks

Escalator and stairway
as inherent elements
of the ring construction

Verglaster Personenaufzug
auf der Galerie

Glazed passenger elevator
on the gallery

Lüftungskonzept

Ventilation Concept

Belüftung mit natürlicher Abluft

Frischluft gelangt über Drallauslässe im Deckenbereich in die Halle. Über Rauch- und Wärmeabzüge kann die Abluft auf natürlichem Wege entweichen.

Kühlfall

Kühle Luft strömt über horizontal eingestellte Drallauslässe in die Halle. Bei besonders hohen Kühllastfällen kann separat erzeugte Kaltluft über Schlauchlutten ins Kanalsystem eingebracht werden (temporäre Zusatzlüftung). Die Abluft der Halle wird zu einem Teil wieder der Zuluft beigemischt.

Heizfall

Erwärmte Luft dringt über vertikal nach unten strömende Drallauslässe in die Halle. Die abgesaugte Luft wird zu einem Teil wieder der Zuluft beigemischt.

Ventilation with Natural Exhaust Air

Fresh air is brought in through twist registers in the ceiling zone. The exhaust air can exit by natural means via smoke and heat flues.

The Cooling Load

Cooled air is blown into the hall through horizontally set twist registers. For especially high cooling loads, separately generated chilled air can be channeled into the duct system (temporary supplementary cooling). Part of the exhaust air from the hall is mixed in with the fresh air supply.

The Heating Load

Heated air is brought into the hall through vertical twist registers directed downward. Part of the exhaust air is mixed in with the fresh air supply.

Belüftung mit
natürlicher Abluft

Ventilation with
natural exhaust

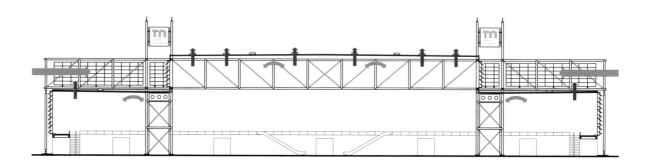

Kühlfall

Cooling load

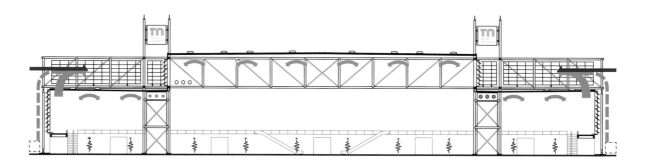

Heizfall

Heating load

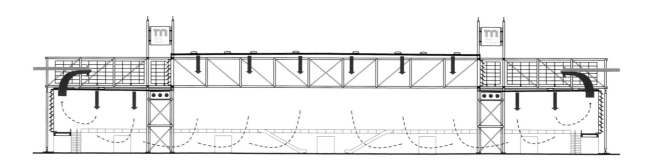

Die Zuluftversorgung erfolgt über acht Lüftungszentralen, die als Auflast auf den Kragarmen der
großen Dachträger angeordnet sind. Das Kanalsystem
im Deckenbereich ist zweigeteilt und versorgt sowohl
den niedrigen als auch den hohen Hallenteil über
gleichmäßig dicht angeordnete elektrisch verstellbare
Drallauslässe.

Die Lüftungsanlagen sind für Veranstaltungen mit
14.000 Personen ausgelegt. Die hohen Anforderungen
für spezielle Messen, wie z.B. die Druck- und Kunst-
stoffmesse erforderte eine maximale spezifische
Kühllast von 300 W/m². Die dann eingeblasene
Zulufttemperatur beträgt 11°C. Beim maximalen
Zuluftvolumenstrom werden in der Grundlüftung
1.200.000 m³/h, mit der temporären Zusatzlüftung
darüber hinaus noch weitere 480.000 m³/h in die Halle
eingeblasen.

The fresh-air supply is brought in from eight ventilation plants that are located upon the cantilevers
of the large roof beams and that act as superimposed
loads. The duct system in the ceiling zone is designed
in two parts and supplies both the lower and the
upper hall area via evenly distributed, electrically
adjustable twist vents.

The ventilation facilities are designed for events with
up to 14,000 people. The high requirements for special
fairs, such as the Printing and Plastics fair, required
a maximum specific cooling load of 300 W/m². The
blown-in air temperature is then 11°C. At maximum
air volume supply 1,200,000 m³/h are blown into
the hall, with an additional 480,000 m³/h with the
temporary supplemental ventilation.

Beleuchtungskonzept

Lighting Concept

Die Halle 6 ist als Tageslichthalle konzipiert, sie kann jedoch auch komplett mit Hilfe der Fassadenlamellen verdunkelt werden. Als Messe- und Veranstaltungshalle ist sie mit einer Grundbeleuchtung von 300 Lux ausgestattet. Um eine gleichmäßige Ausleuchtung zu erzielen, wurden 400 Pendelleuchten als Halogenmetalldampflampen im Deckenbereich in Höhe der Untergurtebene des Raumtragwerks angeordnet. Im Messebetrieb setzen zusätzliche Standleuchten jeden Messestand ins rechte Licht.

Bei einer Farbtemperatur von 3800 Kelvin und einer Farbwiedergabe von RA 80-82 mischt sich das Hallenlicht optimal mit dem TV-Scheinwerferlicht aus Halogenglühlampen. Bodeneinbaustrahler beleuchten die Maststützen sowohl im Hallenraum als auch im Außenbereich vor der Fassade.

Hall 6 is conceived of as a daylight hall that can, however, be completely darkened by its façade louvers. It is equipped with a primary lighting level of 300 lux for trade fairs and other events. In order to achieve an even illumination level, 400 halogen metal halide-hanging lamps were installed in the ceiling zone at the height of the lower space frame chord. During trade fairs additional floor-level lighting complements and enhances each stand.

The hall lighting, with a color temperature of 3800° Kelvin and a color rendering of RA 80-82, mixes optimally with the incandescent halogen lamps of the TV spotlights. Floor-mounted uplights illuminate the columns of the masts in the interior of the hall as well as in the exterior zone in front of the façade.

Beleuchtung bei
verdunkelter Halle

Lighting in the darkened hall

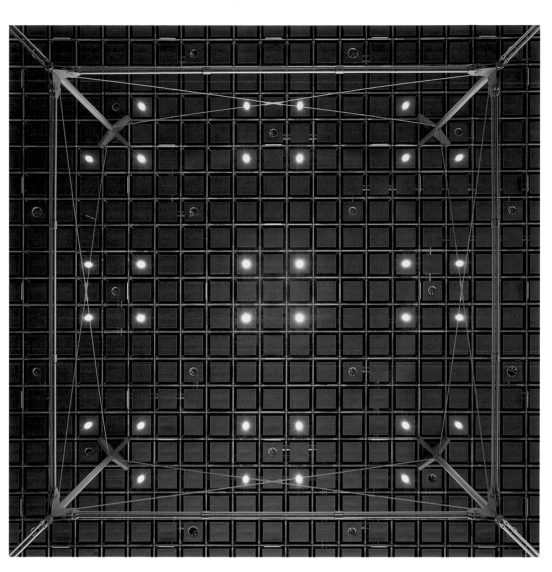

Deckenuntersicht
im Zentrum der Halle

View of the ceiling at
the center of the hall

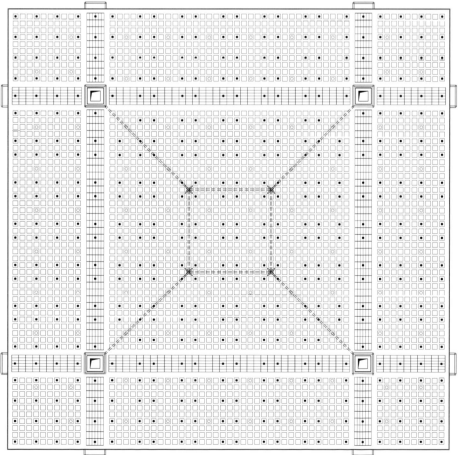

Deckenspiegel mit Beleuchtung
und Lüftungsauslässen

Ceiling plan with lighting
and ventilation registers

Nutzungsvarianten

Variations in Use

Die Halle 6 ist neben ihrer Alltagsbestimmung für Messen und Ausstellungen als multifunktionale Veranstaltungshalle geplant:

Mobile Tribünenanlagen, die als Grundausstattung Bestandteil der Halle sind und die innerhalb eines Tages aufgebaut werden können, ermöglichen eine variable Tribünengestaltung für Konzerte, Shows, Großversammlungen für Politik und Gesellschaft, aber auch für Sportveranstaltungen wie Boxen, Tennis, Fußballturniere und vieles mehr.

Schuhmesse

Shoe fair

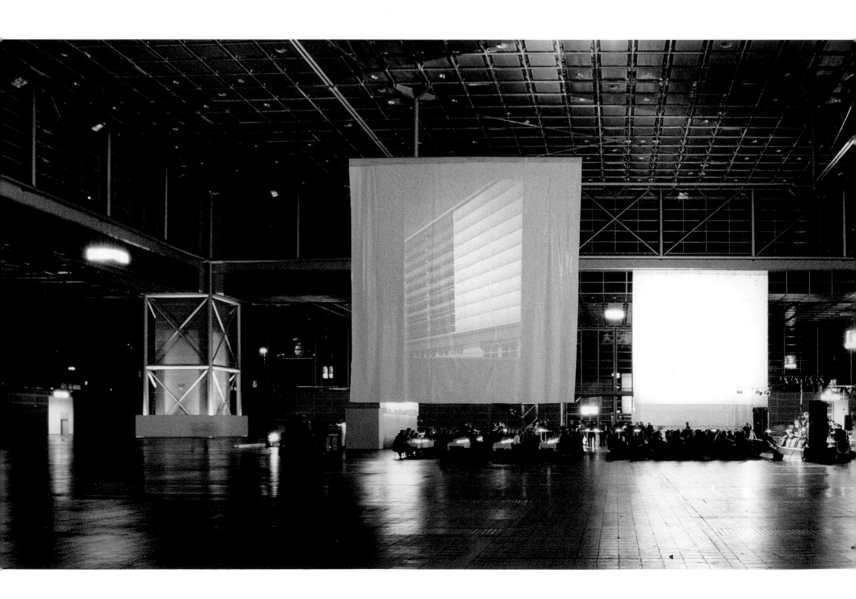

Besides its everyday task of serving trade fairs and exhibitions, Hall 6 is conceived of as a multi-purpose space for shows and performances.

Portable seating stands, which are an integral part of the hall's equipment and which can be set up within one day, enable a flexible seating arrangement for concerts, shows, large gatherings for political or social purposes, as well as for sports events such as boxing, tennis, soccer matches and much more.

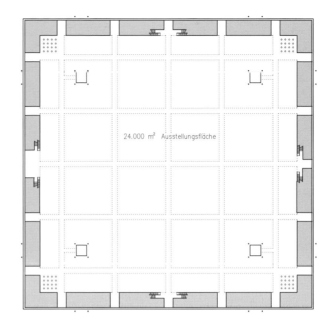

Messe und Ausstellung

Trade fair and exhibition

Konzerthalle

Concert hall

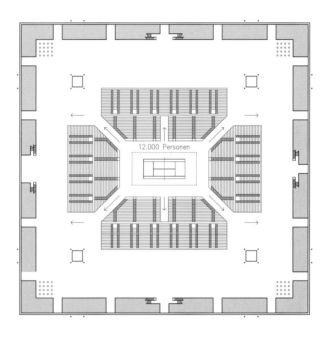

Tennisveranstaltung

Tennis setup

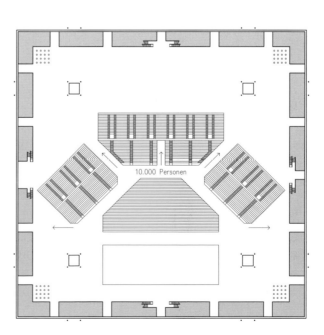

Show und Konzert

Show and concert

Messenutzung
während der ›Boot‹ 2001

Trade fair during
the "Boot" 2001 fair

Ergänzungsbauten

Ancillary Buildings

Im Zuge der durch den Bau der Halle 6 ausgelösten städtebaulichen Neuordnung des nördlichen Messebereichs wurden weitere ergänzende Bauten geplant und zum Teil bereits verwirklicht.

Die Energiezentrale, die die notwendige Heiz- und Kälteleistung für die Halle erzeugt und darüber hinaus Reserven für die technische Aufrüstung der bestehenden Hallen bietet, liegt entlang des künftigen Weges zum geplanten Verbindungsplateau zwischen Rheinstadion und Halle 6. Die verglaste Front gewährt dem Passanten Einblicke in das technische Innenleben mit seiner eigenen Ästhetik.

Die Halle 7 ergänzt den Hallenrundlauf am Nordeingang. Als reine Messehalle orientiert sie sich in Ausstattung und Größe an den bestehenden Hallen. Gestalterisch nimmt sie Bezug auf vorhandene Gliederungselemente und setzt mit exakter Detailausbildung und neuer Farbgebung Akzente.

Das Verbindungsplateau zwischen Rheinstadion und Halle 6 dient einerseits der separaten und vom Messebetrieb unabhängigen Erschließung der Halle bei großen Veranstaltungen, andererseits verbindet es fußläufig Europaplatz und Rheinufer, die durch die künftige Rheinbahntrassierung voneinander getrennt werden. Mit Hilfe der neuen Plattform lassen sich Stadion und Halle im Verbund nutzen.

Am Europaplatz entsteht mit dem Bahnhof Messe Nord die neue Rheinbahnhaltestelle. Der nördliche Messeeingang wird über eine 15 Meter breite Brückenplattform mit dem Europaplatz verbunden.

In the course of the new urban design plan for the northern fair zone set in motion by the construction of Hall 6, further ancillary buildings have been planned and partially built.

The central energy plant, which generates the needed heating and cooling power for the hall, and which also offers reserve capacity for the technical upgrade of the existing halls, lies along the future path to the planned connecting plateau between the Rhine Stadium and Hall 6. The glazed façade offers passersby a glance into the technical "inner life" of the building's unique aesthetic.

Hall 7 complements the hall tour at the north entrance. As a pure trade fair hall it reflects the existing halls with regard to equipment and size. In terms of design, it makes reference to existing elements of articulation and sets accents with exacting detailing and new color concepts.

The connecting plateau between the Rhine Stadium and Hall 6 serves, on the one hand, the separate access to the hall for large events independent of trade fair operations, while on the other hand establishing a pedestrian link between the Europaplatz and the shore of the Rhine. These will be severed from each other in the future by the planned rail right-of-way on the Rhine. The new platform helps to utilize the stadium and the hall in a combined manner.

The "Messe Nord" rail station will serve the new Rhine rail stop at Europaplatz. It will be connected via a 15-meter-wide bridge platform to the northern entrance of the trade fair.

Lageplan im Modell

Site plan in the model

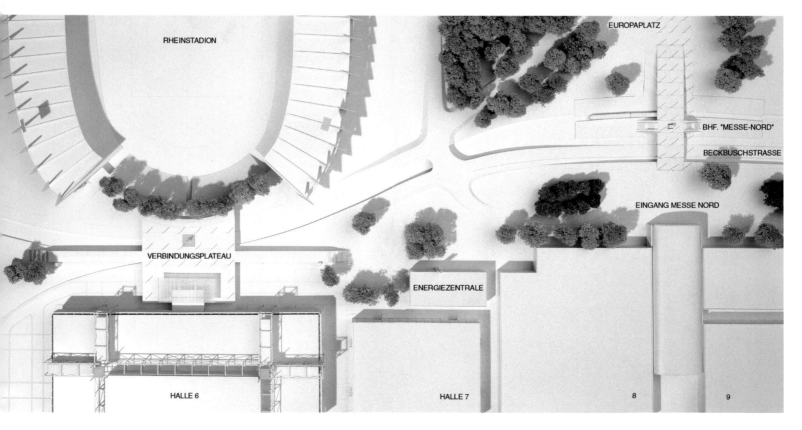

58

Energiezentrale

Bauzeit: März 1999 bis März 2000
Technische Einbauten: Heiz- und Kälteanlagen
Abmessungen: 20 x 30 m
Höhe: 13,70 m

Energy Plant

Dates of construction: March 1999 to March 2000
Technical equipment: Heating and cooling facilities
Measurements: 20 by 30 meters
Height: 13.7 meters

Halle 7

Bauzeit: Oktober 1999 bis März 2000
Ausstellungsfläche: 3.900 m²
Abmessungen: 60 x 75 m
Höhe: 15,50 m

Hall 7

Dates of construction: October 1999 to March 2000
Exhibition area: 3,900 m²
Measurements: 60 by 75 meters
Height: 15.5 meters

Geplantes Verbindungsplateau
zwischen Halle 6
und Rheinstadion

Planned connecting plateau
between Hall 6
and the Rhine Stadium

Projektbeteiligte

**Contributors
to the Project**

Bauherr/Client:

Düsseldorfer Messegesellschaft mbH

Architekten/Architects:

von Gerkan, Marg und Partner, Aachen
Prof. Volkwin Marg
Projektleitung/Project manager: Joachim Rind
Mitarbeiter Wettbewerb/Competition co-workers:
Frederik Jaspert, Marek Nowak, Olaf Drehsen,
Thomas Heuer, Christina Harenberg, Thomas Behr
Mitarbeiter Ausführung/Co-workers construction
planning: Michael Haase, Heiko Körner, Marek Nowak,
Simone Ripp, Stefanie Streb, Petra Tallen,
Andreas Wietheger, Timo Holland, Stephan Menke,
Anne Werrens

Tragwerkplanung/Structural Design:

Schlaich, Bergermann und Partner, Stuttgart
Dr. Michael Pötzl, Knut Göppert, Peter Scheffold,
Michael Werwigk, Nicole Zuber, Hansmartin Fritz

Massivkonstruktionen/Civil Engineering:

Ing. Büro Gehlen, Düsseldorf
Dr. Burkhard Jüdt, Karl Theo Reinhart

Prüfstatik/Statics Control:

Ing. Büro Dr. Kersten, Meerbusch

Haustechnik/Building Services:

HL-Technik AG, Frankfurt
Helmut Langstein, Jürgen Pfaff, Eckehart Bender,
Thomas Golze, Herbert Küster, Gebhard Lodowicks,
Andreas Rehn, Stefan Schwab

Projektsteuerung/Project Management:

Gerd Ehrlicher, Architekten + Ingenieure, Griesheim
Gerd Ehrlicher, Carsten Ferch
Pelège GmbH, Ratingen
Martin Holzschneider

Brandschutz/Fire Protection:

Ing.-Büro Peter Lorsbach, Solingen
Peter Lorsbach

Generalunternehmer/General Contractor:

Arbeitsgemeinschaft Hochtief/Holzmann, Düsseldorf
Matthias Böning, Ulrich Wölfer, Carsten Faust,
Marcel Angenend, Lars Berghoff, Gerd Hebenstreit,
Achim Karrenbauer, Dr. Stefan Jägering, Ingo Magon,
Wilhelm Merschbrock, Goranka Miljesevic,
Bernhard Püschel, Arno Winterboer

Generalunternehmer:
Arbeitsgemeinschaft Hochtief /
Ph. Holzmann

General contractor:
partnership between Hochtief
and Ph. Holzmann

Planungsteam gmp

Gmp planning team

Erster Spatenstich:
Matthias Böning,
Oberbürgermeisterin Smeets,
Hartmut Krebs

First ground-breaking by
Matthias Böning, Mayor
Smeets and Hartmut Krebs

Prof. Volkwin Marg
beim Richtfest

Professor Volkwin Marg
at the topout celebration

Hallenfest:
Prof. Volkwin Marg, Winfried
Moog und Ulrich Wölfer

Hall celebration:
Professor Volkwin Marg,
Winfried Moog
and Ulrich Wölfer

Technische Daten	Außenmaße der Halle	160 x 160 m	Deckenabhängelasten	
	Lichte Höhe Randbereich	16 m	im Raster von 2,50 m	100 kg
Technical Data	Lichte Höhe Innenbereich	24 m	im Raster von 5,00 m	1000 kg
	Größte Stützenfreiheit	90 x 90 m	im Raster von 15,00 m	3000 kg
	Ausstellungsfläche	24.000 m²	Heizleistung	6,6 MW
	Überbaute Fläche	25.600 m²	Kälteleistung	16,5 MW
	Umbauter Raum	630.300 m³	Lüftungsleistung	1.240.000 m³/h
	Bruttogeschossfläche	43.500 m²	Mobile Zusatzlüftung	480.000 m³/h
	Glasfassade	10.500 m²	Elektrische Ausstellerversorgung	350 W/m²
	Erdbewegung	73.000 m³	Beleuchtungsstärke Ausstellerbereich	300 LUX
	Stahlbeton	19.000 m³	Gaststätten – Anzahl Plätze	4 x 75
	Betonstahl	2.750 t	Toranlagen	20
	Stahlmassen	2.300 t	Fahrtreppen	8
	Belastbarkeit des Hallenbodens	100 kN/m	Lasten- und Personenaufzüge	7

Exterior dimensions of the hall	160 x 160 m	Suspended loads from ceiling	
Clear height outer area	16 m	at 2.5 m grid	100 kg
Clear height inner area	24 m	at 5.0 m grid	1000 kg
Largest column-free area	90 x 90 m	at 15.0 m grid	3000 kg
Exhibition area	24,000 m²	Heating capacity	6.6 MW
Building footprint	25,600 m²	Cooling capacity	16.5 MW
Built cubic volume	630,300 m³	Ventilation capacity	1,240,000 m³/h
Gross floor area	43,500 m²	Portable supplemental ventilation	480,000 m³/h
Glass façade	10,500 m²	Electrical exhibition service	350 W/m²
Excavation	73,000 m³	Lighting intensity exhibitor area	300 LUX
Reinforced concrete	19,000 m³	Restaurant seating	4 x 75
Steel reinforcement in concrete	2,750 t	Gates	20
Steel weight	2,300 t	Escalators	8
Maximum floor load in the hall	100 kN/m	Service and passenger elevators	7

Impressum

© Prestel Verlag, München · London · New York
und von Gerkan, Marg und Partner, Hamburg, 2001

Wenn nicht anders angegeben, stammen die Texte von
von Gerkan, Marg und Partner

Auf dem Umschlag: Halle 6, Messe Düsseldorf
Foto: Jürgen Schmidt

Die Deutsche Bibliothek – CIP Einheitsaufnahme
Ein Titelsatz für diese Publikation ist bei der Deutschen
Bibliothek erhältlich

Prestel Verlag
Mandlstraße 26 · 80802 München
Tel. 089/381709-0 · Fax 089/381709-35
www.prestel.de

Lektorat: Stella Sämann
Typographie und Gestaltung: Heinz Ross, München
Reproduktionen: ReproLine GmbH, München
Druck und Bindung: Sellier Druck GmbH, Freising

Gedruckt auf chlorfrei gebleichtem Papier

Printed in Germany
ISBN 3-7913-2579-5

© Prestel Verlag, Munich · London · New York
and von Gerkan, Marg and Partners, Hamburg, 2001

Unless otherwise stated all texts were written by
von Gerkan, Marg and Partners

Translated from the German by Robert Thomas;
Introduction translated by Annette Wiethüchter

Cover: Hall 6, Messe Düsseldorf
Photo: Jürgen Schmidt

Library of Congress Control Number: 200 10 93 012

Prestel Verlag
Mandlstrasse 26 · 80802 Munich
Tel. +49 (89) 381709-0 · Fax + 49 (89) 381709-35;
4 Bloomsbury Place · London WC1A 2QA
Tel. +44 (020) 7323-5004 · Fax +44 (020) 7636-8004;
175 5th Ave., Suite 402 · New York, NY 10010
Tel. +1 (212) 995-2720, Fax +1 (212) 995-2733
www.prestel.com

Prestel books are available worldwide.
Please contact your nearest bookseller or write
to one of the above addresses for information
concerning your local distributor.

Editors: Curt Holtz, Stella Sämann
Typesetting and Design: Heinz Ross, Munich
Lithography: ReproLine GmbH, Munich
Printing and Binding: Sellier Druck GmbH, Freising

Printed in Germany on acid-free paper
ISBN 3-7913-2579-5

Fotonachweis

Photo Credits

(oben/top, Mitte/center, unten/bottom, links/left,
rechts/right)

gmp   51 (links), 56 (oben, unten rechts u. links),
   57 (oben), 60 (unten)
Jörg Hempel   6, 7, 22/23, 35 (unten), 37 (unten), 40,
   47, 56/57, 57 (unten), 58, 59 (unten)
Robert Mehl   51 (rechts), 54/55, 59 (oben u. Mitte),
   61 (unten)
Dr. Michael Pötzl   30, 30/31, 31 (oben u. Mitte)
Jürgen Schmidt   Umschlag, 2, 12, 13, 17, 18, 18/19,
   38, 39, 41, 43, 44 (oben u. unten), 46, 48/49, 53,
   62/63

Andreas Wiese   14/15, 21, 26/27, 45, 52
Messe Düsseldorf: 5 (Rendering)
Delia Dickmann   29, 31 (rechts), 42, 54
Hans Gaspers   28
Axel Schmidt   8/9, 11
n.n.   61 (oben, links u. rechts)

Modellbau/Model design:

Eggers, Aachen   8/9, 11, 22/23, 58, 59 (unten)
Halfmann, Köln   6, 7